# MARTHA'S VINEYARD

## The Delaplaine
## *2022* Long Weekend Guide

**Andrew Delaplaine**

Senior Writer - **James Cubby**

**NO BUSINESS HAS PAID A SINGLE PENNY OR GIVEN *ANYTHING* TO BE INCLUDED IN THIS BOOK.**

Cover Photo by Kate Honish from Pixabay

***MARTHA'S VINEYARD***
**The Delaplaine**
**Long Weekend Guide**

## TABLES OF CONTENTS

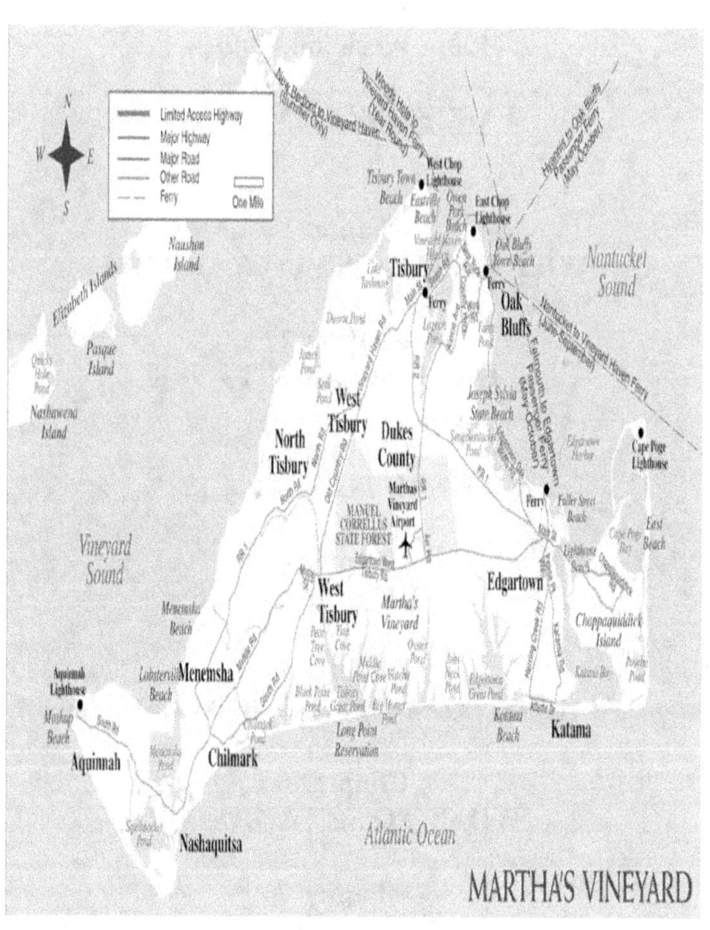
MARTHA'S VINEYARD
Limited Access Highway
Major Highway
Major Road
Other Road
Ferry
One Mile
Nantucket Sound
Vineyard Sound
Atlantic Ocean
Naushon Island
Elizabeth Islands
Pasque Island
Nashawena Island
West Chop Lighthouse
East Chop Lighthouse
Tisbury
Oak Bluffs
North Tisbury
West Tisbury
Dukes County
Martha's Vineyard Airport
MANUEL CORRELLUS STATE FOREST
Edgartown
Cape Poge Lighthouse
Chappaquiddick Island
East Beach
Katama
Katama Beach
Long Point Reservation
Menemsha
Chilmark
Aquinnah
Aquinnah Lighthouse
Nashaquitsa
Joseph Sylvia State Beach
Lobsterville Beach
Menemsha Beach
Martha's Vineyard

# Chapter 1
# WHY MARTHA'S VINEYARD?

The answer is simple—because there's no place quite like it anywhere in America. Yes, you might find some things in common between islands off Georgia or South Carolina, but none of them carry the same *élan* as Martha's Vineyard. The type of people—dare I say the *quality* of people?—that trek to Martha's Vineyard every summer are without doubt the best of the best. It's a little like Sag Harbor, but more of it.

Here on an island that used to be a whaling center you have what some people call "Hollywood East."

You get celebrities, yes, but also writers and academics and practically the entire East Coast Establishment intelligentsia. Conversation in the restaurants and bars always seems elevated to a fascinating level.

On all those other islands—from Pawleys Island to Catalina—people go to get away from it all. Here on Martha's Vineyard, they bring a little of what they left behind with them.

If you spend enough time here, you'll see what I mean. You just meet the most interesting people in the world.

Whether you agree with their views or not is another matter, but that's why it's fun and stimulating to talk to them.

Martha's Vineyard is broken up into 6 towns divided into the two sides of the island called Up Island and Down Island. (Though it would be more accurate for these divisions to be East Island and West Island.)

**UP ISLAND TOWNS**

**AQUINNAH**. The **Gay Head Lighthouse** is out here on the western end.

**CHILMARK**. Still a quaint area with charming fishing villages and boats bobbing in the water.

**WEST TISBURY**. Wild expanses of empty land. You'll be surprised to see there's so much of it still left. Lots of locals are fierce preservationists.

**DOWN ISLAND TOWNS**

**EDGARTOWN**. One of the oldest parts of Martha's Vineyard, here's you'll see beautiful old homes once inhabited by the rich whaling captains.

**OAK BLUFFS**. Tourist Central, though I hate to put it that way. Lots of 19th Century architectural gems here, numerous shops, eateries.

**VINEYARD HAVEN**. The big ferry terminus is here in Vineyard Haven. Lots of great little shops.

# Chapter 2
# GETTING ABOUT

The island is only 7 to 8 miles from Cape Cod, and you can hop a ferry to Martha's Vineyard from Falmouth, Hyannis, Nantucket, New Bedford and Woods Hole in Massachusetts; Quonset Point in Rhode Island, Montauk on Long Island and also New York City.

Ferries from Woods Hole to Martha's Vineyard run year round. Others run seasonally. Check schedules. Full list can be found at www.mvy.com.

If you're bringing your car, you have to use the ferry at Woods Hole. Complete information at www.vineyardferries.com. 508-477-8600. Trip runs 45 minutes.

If you're coming as a passenger from Cape Cod, it runs about an hour from Hyannis on the **Hy-Line,** www.hylinecruises.com. 800-492-8082.
From Falmouth on the **Island Queen** it takes about a half hour: www.islandqueen.com. 508-548-4800.
Once on the island, you can use the pretty efficient bus system that runs all over the place. The Martha's Vineyard Transit Authority, Edgartown, www.vineyardtransit.com - 508-693-9440.

Lots of taxis are also available.

Or you can rent bikes or scooters.

**MARTHA'S VINEYARD BIKE RENTALS**
One Main St, Edgartown, 800-627-2763
Email: marthas@marthasvineyardbikes.com
www.marthasvineyardbike.com
Pick-up and delivery to any island location.

**VINEYARD VEHICLES RENTALS**
Beach Rd, Vineyard Haven, 508-693-1185.

Or rent a car or moped from:

**A-A ISLAND AUTO RENTAL**
800-627-6333, 508-696-5300
info@mvautorental.com
www.mvautorental.com
They have locations in Vineyard Haven, Oak Bluffs and Edgartown.

HOTEL

# Chapter 3
# WHERE TO STAY

***DID YOU FIND AN INTERESTING PLACE?***
If you discover a place you think I should check out on my next visit, drop me a line, will you? I'll mention your name if I end up listing it.
andrewdelaplaine@mac.com

**BEACH PLUM INN**
50 Beach Plum Ln, Chilmark, 508-645-9454
www.beachpluminn.com
They only have a dozen rooms in this charming little inn on a hill overlooking Menemsha Harbor. Superior

views in a wide vista. Lots of bright pastels are used in the rooms. You'll love the alpacas that live on the property. Just as attractive is the restaurant here, also called the **Beach Plum** that has a brief menu that changes daily. (Cucumber soup, Monkfish liver crostini, lamb burger, roasted chicken for 2.)

**CHARLOTTE INN**
27 S Summer St, Edgartown, 508-627-4751
www.thecharlotteinn.com
The 20 rooms here look and feel absolutely nothing like what you're used to. Meaning that they don't feel like "hotel" rooms. They look as if you've been given a lavish guest-room in somebody's large private home. The rooms are so beautifully and painstakingly decorated. Grandfather clocks, antiques in every room, plush bedding and comforters, lots of bric-a-brac. (The quality of the furnishings probably accounts for their "no kids under 14" policy, and I don't blame them one bit.) The white clapboard house

dates from 1864, and obviously belonged to a rich merchant or a whaling captain. Tall linden trees rise outside. (Those of you who know the place will be well aware the restaurant management changes here every now and then, but it's always an elegant place to dine. Get the lemon pot de crème, the lobster-guacamole starter, blue cheese and fig risotto. Also, they warn you about a strict dress code, but it's not always enforced.

**THE DOCKSIDE INN**
9 Circuit Ave, Oak Bluffs, 800-245-5979
www.vineyardinns.com
Only 21 rooms in this boutique style property where everything is tastefully elegant. It's just a few feet from the Oak Bluffs ferry terminal, and from their wide wraparound porches, you can see boats making their way in and out of the harbor. They have a 1956 Rolls Royce Silver Cloud they use as a courtesy car.

**HARBOR VIEW HOTEL**
131 N Water St, Edgartown, 508-627-7000
www.harborviewhotel.com
This historic property went up in 1891, and they still have the rocking chairs on the wide porches to prove it. Great views, personal service, open year-round. I like the rooms in the old main building, but they have more modern lodgings in their Governor Mayhew Building. They also have cottages and suites in another building. (In fact, they offer such a wide choice of lodgings you'd do well to look into them all before deciding what to book.) Has an excellent dining room and a very nice bar, **Henry's Hotel Bar**. Again, since they're open around the year, this is a perfect place to spend a romantic weekend—yes, even in the winter.

**HOB KNOB**
128 Main St, Edgartown, 508-627-9510
www.hobknob.com
Love the name of this charming B&B with its relaxing porches and cozy lobby with a fireplace they use in the winter. (There's a history about the name, but you'll find that out when you get here.) They offer 17 plush rooms, comfortably decorated, and not as "fuddy-duddy" as some of the other, older inns. (They also have 2 houses for rent year round, the Tilton House and Thaxter House—these houses have kitchens a gourmet would love to work in, so they make good choices if you want to cook.) They're proud to say they are an "eco-lodging," and your breakfast and afternoon tea are made with ingredients supplied by local farms. Business center services, spa

treatments, fitness room, sauna & steam. They also have a Boston Whaler you can use to go out to survey the Vineyard from the water—or go fishing.

**MARTHA'S VINEYARD RESORT**

111 New York Ave, Oak Bluffs, 800-874-4403

NO WEBSITE

Has 6 nice rooms and 2 suites. The rooms are a little small and somewhat Spartan, but suitable. Very convenient to everything. Large lobby is great for meeting other guests or entertaining friends.

**WINNETU OCEANSIDE RESORT**
31 Dunes Rd, Edgartown, 508-310-1733
www.winnetu.com
The 54-suite Winnetu is as close as the Vineyard gets to a mega-resort, with a library, fitness center, and vast lawn outfitted with a nine-hole putting green and a turtle pond. The hotel is just a 250-yard walk from the beach.

# Chapter 4
# WHERE TO EAT

***DID YOU FIND AN INTERESTING PLACE?***

If you discover a place you think I should check out on my next visit, drop me a line, will you? I'll mention your name if I end up listing it.

andrewdelaplaine@mac.com

Many restaurants close in the winter off-season and others trim their hours. Check to make sure.

Only 2 towns allow alcohol to be sold: Edgartown and Oak Bluffs. Vineyard Haven has jumped in and now lets restaurants serve beer and wine (but no hard liquor), and then you have to have food served as well.

These are odd rules you expect in backwater counties in North Carolina, but not up here. Anyway, in the other towns, West Tisbury, Chilmark and Aquinnah, you have to BYOB.

**7A FOODS**

1045 State Rd, West Tisbury, (508) 693-4636

www.7afoods.com

CUISINE: Breakfast/Sandwiches

DRINKS: No Booze

SERVING: Breakfast & Lunch, Closed Sundays

PRICE RANGE: $$

Take-out spot focusing on breakfast and lunch – fresh baked goods and sandwiches. Order from the blackboard menu on the wall behind the counter. Favorites: Chicken Salad Sandwich and a concoction they call the Liz Lemon (sandwich with pastrami, turkey, Swiss, coleslaw and Russian dressing, very satisfying, I promise). Also, a mini-market offering staples like milk, eggs, and cheese. The sea salt they sell here is made on the island, as are a lot of the jams and other items they have on offer.

**ALCHEMY BISTRO & BAR**
71 Main St, Edgartown, 508-627-9999
www.alchemyedgartown.com
CUISINE: Seafood, New American
DRINKS: Full bar
SERVING: Dinner
PRICE RANGE: $$$
This classy joint gets loud, but it's FUN. The bar serves up inventive sophisticated specialty cocktails. Try the flash fried zucchini matchsticks. Later, go for the pan-fried halibut with crispy skin or the soft shell crabs with a cornmeal breading.

**AMONG THE FLOWERS CAFÉ**
17 Mayhew Ln, Edgartown, 508-627-3233
No Website
CUISINE: American
DRINKS: Beer & Wine Only
SERVING: Breakfast, Lunch, & Dinner
PRICE RANGE: $$

Just a block from the Edgartown harbor is this popular small café offering a menu of comfort food standards including delicious sandwiches and salads. Get a seat in the brick patio where there's plenty of shade in the summer. Great breakfast pick. Favorites include: Lobster rolls and Turkey & Swiss sandwich. Gluten-free options available.

**ART CLIFF DINER**
39 Beach Rd, Vineyard Haven, 508-693-1224

www.artcliffdiner.com
CUISINE: American
DRINKS: No Booze
SERVING: Breakfast, Lunch
PRICE RANGE: $$
Retro diner offering a menu of American classics. It has those old-time swivel stools at the lunch counter, and I've hated them all my life, almost as long as this place has been open, which is decades. But I put up with them because the diner food is so damn good.

**ATLANTIC FISH & CHOP HOUSE**
2 Main St, Edgartown, 508-627-7001
www.atlanticmv.com
CUISINE: Seafood
DRINKS: Full Bar
SERVING: Lunch, Dinner
PRICE RANGE: $$$
Casual eatery that feels more like a yacht club (because of its lively bar scene) than a restaurant. Great menu of steaks and seafood. Favorites include: Tuna tartare and Lobster roll. Hangout on the second-level deck.

**BACK DOOR DONUTS**

1-11 Kennebec Ave, Oak Bluffs, 508-693-3688
www.backdoordonuts.com
CUISINE: Bakery
DRINKS: No Booze
SERVING: 7 pm till after midnight in summer. (Has seasonal hours—check first)
PRICE RANGE: $

Nondescript back door in a parking lot attracts long lines when it opens after the sun goes down. Bakery offers an impressive selection of donuts, oversized apple fritters (for which they're famous), cookies, eclairs, cannolis, croissants, fruit squares, fruit turnovers, and scones. All this served out the back door. Note: there's usually a long line waiting. They also serve sandwiches.

**BARN BOWL & BISTRO**
13 Uncas Ave, Oak Bluffs, 508-696-9800
www.thebarnmv.com
CUISINE: New American (Bowling Alley)
DRINKS: Full bar
SERVING: Lunch & Dinner – year-round
PRICE RANGE: $$
Busy bowling alley (10 regulation lanes) with a bright and cheery bar and eatery (that while it overlooks the lanes, is soundproofed so the noise doesn't ruin your time eating) serving burgers, pizza, and other nibbles. Favorites: BBQ Chicken Pizza and Fish sandwich.

**THE BLACK DOG TAVERN**
20 Beach St Extension, Vineyard Haven, 508-693-9223
www.theblackdog.com
CUISINE: Seafood, American
DRINKS: Beer & Wine Only
SERVING: Breakfast (from 7), Lunch & Dinner
PRICE RANGE: $$

This is quite a place. You'll notice their logo plastered all over the island. The inside is decorated with a wondrous array of nautical artifacts, everything from netting to tackle, buoys, oars—you get the idea. It's just that there's so much of it. Sit outside at a picnic table and take in the splendid waterfront view. You're really here for the view. Service is spotty and the food is OK, most especially the lobster mac & cheese, the chowders, the egg dishes in the morning.

**COPPER WOK**
9, Main St, Vineyard Haven, 508-693-3416
www.copperwokmv.com
CUISINE: Sushi/Japanese
DRINKS: Full bar
SERVING: Lunch & Dinner
PRICE RANGE: $$
Modern eatery offering a menu of creative sushi rolls, Asian entrees and sake cocktails.
Favorites: Chicken Shu Mai, Fried Pork Dumplings and Coconut Green Curry Shrimp.

**DETENTE RESTAURANT AND WINE BAR**
15 Winter St, Edgartown, 508-627-8810
www.detentemv.com
CUISINE: New American
DRINKS: Full bar
SERVING: Dinner
PRICE RANGE: $$$
Modern, sophisticated seasonal kitchen offering a menu of fresh local products. Plates are very professional and stylishly prepared. Gorgeous. Small portions. Not the place to come if you're starving.
Favorites: Lobster Ravioli and Hand rolled pastas.

Extensive wine list. Nice romantic patio out back in-season.

**ESPRESSO LOVE**
17 Church St (behind the courthouse), Edgartown, 508-627-9211
www.espressolove.com
CUISINE: Coffee shops; Sandwiches & Salads
DRINKS: No booze
SERVING: Breakfast (from 6), lunch till 6 p.m.
PRICE RANGE: $
Great selection of fresh baked goods, good breakfast items, hearty sandwiches and entrée sized salads for lunch. But the COFFEE is a big attraction here, too. Lots of celebs show up here. But there's room for you, too. Very friendly. Christina Thornton (chef-owner of **Hooked**), starts her morning here with an iced coffee.

**GIORDANO'S CLAM BAR**
18 Lake Ave, Oak Bluffs, 508-693-0184
www.giosmv.com
CUISINE: Pizza
DRINKS: Full Bar
SERVING: Lunch, Dinner
PRICE RANGE: $$
Open for over 80 years, this place is known for its family style Italian classics and pizza. (The whole fried clams are a standout.) Carry-out window offers a take-away option for those looking for a quick lunch.

**GRACE EPISCOPAL CHURCH LOBSTER ROLLS (Fridays Only)**

36 Woodlawn Ave, Vineyard Haven, 508 693-0332
www.graceepiscopalmv.org/
CUISINE: Lobster Rolls
DRINKS: No Booze
SERVING: Dinner – seasonal hours
PRICE RANGE: $

It's hard to find a real bargain on expensive Cape Cod, but here's one. A Stuffed Lobster roll dinner for a very cheap price here at Grace. It's Fridays only (4 – 7:30), and runs in the summer, usually through the end of September. You get the lobster roll, chips, a drink, sometimes even dessert, when they have it. Other foods served – hot dogs and dessert. Eat in the rec hall or take it to go. Funds go to island non-profits. Arrive early. The secret is out on this place, LOL.

**LARSEN'S FISH MARKET**
56 Basin Rd, Chilmark, 508-645-2680
www.larsensfishmarket.com
CUISINE: American
DRINKS: No Booze
SERVING: Breakfast (from 9), lunch & early dinner (till 7)
PRICE RANGE: $
In the fishing village of Menemsha. It is a great spot for clams or oysters on the half shell and to watch the sunset. (**Menemsha Beach** is one of the few places you can actually watch the sun set into the water.) Though the big deal here is the fresh fish for sale in the market, their kitchen will cook to order these items: Lobster, Chowder of the Day, Lobster Bisque, Stuffed Quahogs, Stuffed Scallops, Crab Cakes,

Steamers, Mussels. The seafood here is about an unadorned, unfancy and GOOD as you can get.

**LITTLE HOUSE CAFÉ**

339 State Rd, Vineyard Haven, 508-687-9794

www.littlehousemv.com

CUISINE: Mediterranean/American (Traditional)

DRINKS: Full bar

SERVING: B'fast, Lunch, & Dinner, Closed Sundays; this place closes for an hour between b'fast & lunch (11-11:30) and lunch & dinner (4 to 5), just so you know.

PRICE RANGE: $$

Cozy little café (just simple wooden chairs & tables, nothing fancy) serving international and American cuisine to a host of locals as well as the tourist who know enough to come here. Gluten-free and vegetarian options. Favorites: Fish tacos, curried mango chicken salad sandwich and Nonna's meatballs. Desserts are all homemade.

**MENEMSHA FISH MARKET**

54 Basin Rd, Chilmark, 508-645-2282
http://www.menemshafishmarket.net
CUISINE: Seafood Market
DRINKS: Full bar
SERVING: 10 a.m. – 5 p.m.
PRICE RANGE: $$

Seafood market selling fresh seafood – local and international. Menu mainly features fresh seafood dishes coming from their own market, everything from lobsters to red snapper, little necks, scallops and clam chowder. Good soups, sandwiches. Eat outside on the dock overlooking the fishing boats. Delivery available.

**PORT HUNTER**
55 Main St, Edgartown, 508-627-7747
www.theporthunter.com
CUISINE: Seafood
DRINKS: Full Bar
SERVING: Dinner
PRICE RANGE: $$S
Very friendly eatery that's so relaxed they offer tables for standing and regular seating. The décor matches the seafood-focused menu. Menu favorites include: Quinoa fritters, fish tacos, Chatham mussels in a spicy curry sauce, Buffalo Brussels sprouts served with a blue cheese mousse. Music later. Great cocktails and shuffleboard.

**RED CAT KITCHEN**
14 Kennebec Ave, Oak Bluffs, 508-696-6040
www.redcatkitchen.com
CUISINE: American (New)/Seafood
DRINKS: Full Bar

SERVING: Dinner
PRICE RANGE: $$$
A very welcoming atmosphere greets you here, whether you eat inside where you can enjoy art created by locals or outside on the porch beneath the Chinese lanterns. This place offers a very creative menu with names to match. Try the Island Fresca – a Parmesan soup with island corn, tomatoes, and basil that is quite famous locally. The dishes come with a great medley of local vegetables that makes every dish special.

**SCOTTISH BAKEHOUSE**
977 State Rd, Vineyard Haven, 508-693-6633
www.scottishbakehousemv.com
CUISINE: American
DRINKS: No Booze
SERVING: Breakfast, lunch, dinner

PRICE RANGE: $$

More to this place than meets the eye. Take a look at the garden out back—a lot of the food they serve here comes from it. Egg sandwich for b'fast is only $4; full line of sandwiches for lunch, hefty wraps; entrees include quesadilla; spicy peanut noodles; Brazilian plate; kale & sweet potato mash; soups, salads, all fresh, fresh, fresh. (They go through 100 pounds of kale every week in season.) Specialty menu items for you if you're vegan, a carnivore, localvore, baconitarian, gluten free, sugar-free, you name it. Open year round.

**STATE ROAD**

688 State Rd, West Tisbury, 508-693-8582
www.stateroadmv.com
CUISINE: Diners
DRINKS: No Booze
SERVING: Breakfast, lunch, dinner
PRICE RANGE: $$$

The Obamas liked this place, and so will you. Try the bacon cheddar Jalapeno grits for breakfast. (Hot!) Or the hash that changes daily. Lunch from 11 till 2: sandwiches and salads. Dinner (from 5:30) offers treats like sugar snap pea salad, shrimp & grits and lobster salad for starters, and items like loin of rabbit, lamb chops or prosciutto wrapped monkfish for main courses. Very nice spot. They have gardens out back that supply lots of the ingredients served here. This is a relatively new place on the Vineyard, but it still has a "tavern" feel to it, with wood beams and rustic chandeliers giving off a cozy glow.

**THE SWEET LIFE CAFE**
63 Circuit Ave, Oak Bluffs, 508-696-0200
www.sweetlifemv.com
CUISINE: American
DRINKS: Full Bar
SERVING: Dinner
PRICE RANGE: $$$$
Elegant spot with prices to match in this Victorian house offering up a romantic setting you'll love the minute you walk in. Great tuna tartare and very creative soups. The meats are top quality: lamb sirloin, breaded quail breast, dry-rubbed rib eye. (You can get seafood a hundred other places, right?) Has one of the better wine lists on the island.

# Chapter 5
# WHERE TO SHOP
# (& SERVICES)

***DID YOU FIND AN INTERESTING PLACE?***

If you discover a place you think I should check out on my next visit, drop me a line, will you? I'll mention your name if I end up listing it.

andrewdelaplaine@mac.com

**ALLEN WHITING GALLERY**

985 State Rd, West Tisbury, 508-693-4691

allenwhiting.com
Gallery exhibiting the work of local artist Allen Whiting – known for his oil paintings featuring locales in the surrounding area.

**ALLEY'S GENERAL STORE**
1045 State Rd, West Tisbury, 508-693-0088
www.mvpreservation.org/properties/alleys-general-store/
This wonderful place has a sign out front that says "Dealers in Almost Everything," and it's been here since 1858. It's always been a general store, so it's the kind of place where you get everything you need, kind of like an old fashioned 7-11 or convenience store. Must stop if you're in West Tisbury.

**BESPOKE ABODE**
56 Main St, Vineyard Haven, 508-687-9555
www.bespokeabode.com
This comfortable shop has lots of items for the home, especially if you're looking for that island feel. Interior designer Liz Stiving-Nichols chooses everything: unusual picture frames, mirrors, pillows, some furniture.

**CHICKEN ALLEY**
38 Lagoon Pond Rd, Vineyard Haven, 508-693-2278.
www.chickenalley.org/
Unique thrift shop that is also part art gallery. A favorite of anybody who likes funky clothing. Shelves of used books, clothing, household items, furniture, artwork and collectibles. The shop hosts the annual Chicken Alley Art's and Collectible Sale on the 2nd Sunday in August.

**THE CHILMARK COFFEE COMPANY**
12 Lagemann Ln, Chilmark, 508-560-1061
chilmarkcoffeeco.com
Todd Christy has dedicated himself to creating the best coffee in the region and his coffees are sold all over the island. This is where it all starts.

**CHILMARK GENERAL STORE**
7 State Rd, Chilmark, 508-645-3739
www.chilmarkgeneralstore.com
An old-fashioned market is a locals' meeting place and a great stop for lunch. The market sells island-grown produce, coffee, household necessities, and almost anything that you might need. Great sandwiches and fresh organic coffee. Grab a slice of their famous pizza and eat it on the porch.

**FIELD GALLERY**
1050 State Rd, West Tisbury, 508-693-5595
www.fieldgallery.com
This gallery has been exhibiting the work of island artists for over 35 years and continues to feature a group of talented artists. Rotating exhibitions of contemporary paintings, sculpture, photography, and other works. Artists' receptions are held Sunday afternoons throughout the summer.

**GRANARY GALLERY**

636 Old Country Rd, West Tisbury, 508-693-0455

www.granarygallery.com

Not your typical gallery geared to tourists featuring "island-y" paintings by local artists. This place features high-end art, with the price tags to match—sculpture, photos, and paintings—by some 70+ big name international artists. (A few locals are represented as well.) Owners are the discerning Christopher and Sheila Morse.

**MARTHA'S VINEYARD GLASSWORKS**
683 State Rd, West Tisbury, 508-693-6026
www.mvglassworks.com
The glass works of 6 or 7 artists are on sale here in this fine shop, from platters to bowls, tableware, jars, vases, display pieces. Here you'll find any number of inventive pieces that will make a great addition to your home (or even your office) or as a gift.

**MERMAID FARM & DAIRY**
9 Middle Rd, Chilmark, 508-645-3492
www.facebook.com/Mermaid-Farm-and-Dairy-371138872899/
Founded in 1997, this 35-acre farm and dairy sells a variety of vegetables, raw milk, handmade yogurt, feta cheese, wheat and rye flours, beef, lamb and pork. Worth a visit.

**NORTH TABOR FARM**
4 North Tabor Farm Rd, Chilmark, 508-645-3311.
www.northtaborfarm.com/
A six-acre farm run by Rebecca Miller with a farm stand on premises selling fresh items like salad greens, eggs, pork, poultry, mushrooms, honey, and flowers.

**TEA LANE FARM**
161 Middle Rd, Chilmark, 774-563-8274
tealanefarm.com
Historic farm owned by the town of Chilmark. Krishana Collins sells her gorgeous flowers at the local farmers' market. Her services are available for weddings, special events, and flower services. The beautiful farm is ideal for hiking, mountain biking and dog walking.

**VINEYARD VINES**
27 N Water St, Edgartown, 508-627-4779
www.vineyardvines.com
Great books, gifts, polo shirts, lots of gifts focusing on the Vineyard.

**WEST TISBURY FARMERS MARKET**
1067 State Road, West Tisbury, 508-693-9561
www.wtfmarket.org
Runs from Jun – Oct, Wed & Sat, 9 – noon, rain or shine. The fruits and vegetables you can buy here come from people on the Vineyard who grew them. Lots of fun. (They also have an abbreviated winter market.) Questions? Contact Linda Alley at 508-693-9561, or email linda@newlanesundries.com

# Chapter 6
# WHAT TO SEE & DO

***DID YOU FIND AN INTERESTING PLACE?***
If you discover a place you think I should check out on my next visit, drop me a line, will you? I'll mention your name if I end up listing it.
andrewdelaplaine@mac.com

**AQUINNAH BEACH**
**MOSHUP BEACH / NUDE BEACH**
www.mvy.com

On the west side of the island is this nice public beach with some parking. Here you'll get to see the cliffs of clay, which rise straight up from the long stretch of lonely beach. (Plan on walking.) The nude section of the beach is at the north end.

**THE CAMPGROUND**

Oak Bluffs, 508-693-0525
www.mvcma.org
Email: office@mvcma.org
Here they have an organization called the Martha's Vineyard Camp Meeting Association (MVCMA), that is quite interesting and well worth your time to look into. They have numerous activities and events in the summer season. There are dozens of Victorian gingerbread cottages. While the cottages were ostensibly built by devout Methodists who set up "camps" when they met here, beginning as far back as 1835, there's been a lot of restoration. Once a year they do a Grand Illumination (I know, it sounds like something from another world) when they hang colorful Japanese and Chinese lanterns in all the cottages. (Usually in the middle of August.) Fun place for the whole family.

**CEDAR TREE NECK SANCTUARY**

Vineyard Haven
www.sheriffsmeadow.org
Here you will find a lovely preserved area that offers splendid relaxed views of forestry, a pond and the ocean beyond. Cedar Creek is maintained by the Sheriff's Meadow Foundation, which has an interesting history. Over in Edgartown, Sheriff Isaiah

Pease owned a meadow that came to be known as Sheriff's Meadow. On it there was a pond used in the winter to cut ice for storage later in the year. Henry Beetle Hough, the editor of the local "Vineyard Gazette," lived nearby and his windows looked out onto the meadow. When he heard the area was going to be developed, he used $7,000, the advance for a book from a New York publisher, to buy the meadow and preserve it. When none of the other preservation groups wanted to take the property, he and wife Elizabeth launched the Sheriff's Meadow Foundation, which now boasts many other areas of Martha's Vineyard that will be preserved for years to come.

**CHAPPAQUIDDICK**

You can jump on a ferry to Chappaquiddick, which is only 300 yards off the Vineyard's east coast. Here you can enjoy miles of empty beaches (depending on the time of year and day you go). Bird watchers flock here to look at spot blue herons, sandpipers and the like.

**DR. DANIEL FISHER HOUSE**

99 Main St, Edgartown, 508-627-4440
https://vineyardtrust.org/
Built in 1840, this Federal style residence is open for visitors and available for weddings and such.

**EDGARTOWN LIGHTHOUSE**

In Edgartown Harbor
www.mvmuseum.org/edgartown.php
In front of the **Harbor View Hotel**, take the path off N Water St.

**FISHING WITH JENNIFER CLARKE**
Chilmark, 508-776-7286
captainclarkecharters.com
Jennifer Clarke, also a successful singer/songwriter, offers a wide variety of charter fishing excursions. Climb aboard Captain Clarke's 30-foot center console charter vessel "Femme Fatale" for what I promise you will be a memorable experience. Martha's Vineyard is a fisherman's paradise boasting the best in striped bass, bluefish, bonito, false albacore, fluke and sea bass fishing.

**FLYING HORSES CAROUSEL**
15 Oak Bluffs Ave, Oak Bluffs, 508-693-9481
www.mvpreservation.org
Open from Easter Sunday through Columbus Day. This is one of the oldest carousels in America and a national landmark, and you just have to see it, even if you don't take a ride. Its horses were hand-carved in 1876 in New York City, one of 2 known carousels

built by Charles W. F. Dare. In 1884, the Flying Horses were brought from Coney Island to Martha's Vineyard and have been operating on the same site for more than a century. Rides are cheap. (And if you catch the brass ring you can get a free ride.)

**GAY HEAD LIGHTHOUSE**
15 Aquinnah Circle, Aquinnah, 508-645-9954
Tues-Sat, mid-June through mid-Sept.
www.gayheadlight.org

**GREAT ROCK BIGHT PRESERVE**
37 Brickyard Rd, Chilmark, 508-627-7141
mvlandbank.com

Owned by the Martha's Vineyard Land bank, this preserve is free to visit. The preserve features many trails and access to 1,300 feet of beach along the Vineyard Sound. The preserve is used for nature study, hiking, picnicking, mountain-biking, horseback riding, hunting (with permission), fishing, and swimming.

**ISLAND ALPACA**

1 Head of Pond Rd, Vineyard Haven, 508-693-5554
www.islandalpaca.com

They breed alpacas here on this 20-acre farm. You can feed the critters and take them for walks. But you'll definitely want to visit the gift store with its clothes for babies, footwear, handbags, totes, purses, jackets, coats, hats, headbands sweaters, scarves, shawls—all made of alpaca here on Martha's Vineyard.

**JAWS BRIDGE**

Seaview Ave, Edgartown

If you want to see what MV looked like in 1975 (and see what's changed and how much hasn't), take a look at Steven Spielberg's 1975 film, "Jaws."

The film crew descended on Edgartown with their 24-foot shark and took the place over for a few months. You'll see lots of houses, stores and other locations in the movie that are still here.

Jaws Bridge is officially the **American Legion Memorial Bridge**, but locals refer to it as **Big Bridge**. It's part of Seaview Avenue, which connects Edgartown with the town of Oak Bluffs. The bridge also divides the Atlantic Ocean from Sengekontacket Pond.

Despite its nickname, the bridge is a small one, just a few car-lengths in total, and it has been refurbished in recent years. The stone quay Roy Scheider ran during the Jaws attack at the bridge is still there and runs perpendicular to the bridge. The beach on the ocean side, called Joseph Sylvia State Beach, was where the rest of the scene was filmed.

**LIGHTHOUSE BEACH**
Water St, Edgartown, 508-627-6145
No Website
You can get spectacular views of Chappaquiddick from the top of this 45-foot high cast iron lighthouse after climbing the spiral staircase. Originally built in 1881 and installed at Ipswich, Mass., it was taken apart and brought here after the lighthouse in Edgartown was damaged in a hurricane.

**LONG POINT WILDLIFE REFUGE**
Hughe's Thumb Rd, 508-693-7392

Off the Edgartown – West Tisbury Road
www.thetrustees.org/places-to-visit/cape-cod-islands/long-point.html
Salt and freshwater ponds, hundreds of acres of beautiful virgin beachfront. At more than 600 acres, Long Point is one of the largest publicly accessible properties on Martha's Vineyard. It encompasses beach, dune, and woodland that surround a broad (and uncommon) sand plain heath. While busy in season, the refuge is especially fun in the winter. (Birdwatchers love it.)

**THE MARTHA'S VINEYARD MUSEUM**
151 Lagoon Pond Rd, Vineyard Haven, 508-627-4441
www.marthasvineyardhistory.org
Authoritative source for history and genealogy on the island. Excellent exhibits including the Thomas

Cooke house, the Francis Foster Museum, the Captain Francis Pease House and Carriage Shed with coverage of whaling and Wampanoag history as well. Modest admission.

**OLD WHALING CHURCH**

89 Main St, Edgartown, 508-627-4442
https://vineyardtrust.org/property/old-whaling-church/
Built by whaling captains in 1843, this landmark is considered on of the finest examples of Greek Revival architecture in New England.

**MENEMSHA BEACH**

Basin Rd, Chilmark
Just a couple of minutes' walk from the fishing village that gives this beach its name, you'll find perhaps the BEST sunset on Martha's Vineyard.

**VINCENT HOUSE MUSEUM**
99 A Main St, Edgartown, 508-627-8017
https://vineyardtrust.org/property/vincent-house-gardens/
Built in 1672, this is probably the oldest standing house on Martha's Vineyard. The museum houses furnishings that show examples of Puritan life to the more elegant Whaling era.

# Chapter 7
# NIGHTLIFE

Nightlife options are somewhat limited by the nature of Martha's Vineyard. In addition, only 2 towns allow alcohol to be sold: Edgartown and Oak Bluffs. Vineyard Haven has jumped in and now lets restaurants serve beer and wine (but no hard liquor), and then you have to have food served as well.

These are odd rules you expect in backwater counties in North Carolina, but not up here. Anyway, in the other towns, West Tisbury, Chilmark and Aquinnah, you have to BYOB.

Some of these are really restaurants, but because they have a lively bar scene, I've put them here to "create" a nightlife" section.

**OFFSHORE ALE CO**

30 Kennebec Ave, Oak Bluffs, 508-693-2626

www.offshoreale.com

This locals' pub is also the only brewery on Martha's Vineyard, and as easily could be in the "What To See & Do" chapter. As such, it's better as a nightlife destination, there being so few places to go here on Martha's Vineyard at night. Toss those peanut shells right on the floor. They don't care. Get the Offshore Amber Ale that's made right there on the premises.

**RITZ CAFÉ**
4 Circuit Ave, Oak Bluffs, 508-693-9851
www.theritzmv.com
On the dock you'll find this dive bar that has live music nightly during season (but off season only on weekends).

**SHARKY'S CANTINA**
31 Circuit Ave, Oak Bluffs, 508-693-7501
266 Upper Main St, Edgartown, 508-627-6565
www.sharkyscantina.com
They boast "50 menu items under $10," so this is a good place to bring the kids. But the bar is busy at night.

# INDEX

S



T



U



V



W

# NOTES

# NOTES

# NOTES

www.ingramcontent.com/pod-product-compliance
Lightning Source LLC
Chambersburg PA
CBHW052229150726
48002CB00003B/1346

* 9 7 9 8 2 0 1 3 2 2 4 9 6 *